Soldiers Fotofax

UNION FORCES
OF THE
AMERICAN CIVIL WAR
Philip Katcher

Front cover illustration:
This cannon crew wears light artillery dress uniform jackets. The number three man, second from left, "thumbs the vent," stopping it with a leather thumbstall so the piece can be reloaded without fear of discharge by the number one man, who is holding the rammer. The number two man holds a tool used to search for pieces of burning powder bags which may be left after firing. The gun is a 6-pound Napoleon.

Back cover illustrations:
Top left: This historian wears the dress uniform of a cavalry corporal, complete with brass shoulder scales and dress hat. The broad black leather strap with the brass buckle hooks to his carbine so it will not be lost while riding. The gloves were not issued, but most men tried to get a pair for field use. Note the black leather sabre knot, worn around the wrist in combat.

Top right: Most volunteers of 1861 arrived in unique unit uniforms. H. Michael Madaus, a Milwaukee Public Museum curator, wears a Wisconsin state uniform of that period and carries the regimental colour of the 2nd Wisconsin Infantry. The state managed to get all its troops into blue uniforms by February 1862, not until some had fought the First Bull Run in grey.

1. Major General Nathaniel Prentiss Banks wears the full dress uniform of his rank, complete with buttons in threes, gold epaulettes, and black velvet collar and cuffs. His sword is a non-regulation presentation model and his sword-belt is gold and black. Banks was a poor general, being driven out of the Shenandoah Valley by Stonewall Jackson in 1862 and thereafter commanding at the badly conducted campaigns of Port Hudson and Red River before being replaced.

UNION FORCES
OF THE
AMERICAN CIVIL WAR

Philip Katcher

ARMS AND
ARMOUR

3. Major General J. Watts DePeyster served in the New York Militia. He holds a peakless pillbox cap which came into use during the war. His two silver stars are embroidered directly on to the uniform coat, without the black background or gold edging used in regulation shoulder-straps. This practice became popular for field use as officers so marked were less obvious to enemy sharpshooters.

▲2

2. Major General Philip Sheridan was one of the Union Army's three greatest generals, the other two being Grant and Sherman. He wears undress shoulder-straps with a silver star at each end. An 1853 West Point graduate, Sheridan had reached the rank of major general by March 1863 and ended the war in command of the Army of the Shenandoah.

3▼

INTRODUCTION

First published in Great Britain in 1989 by Arms and Armour Press, Artillery House, Artillery Row, London SW1P 1RT.

Distributed in the USA by Sterling Publishing Co. Inc., 2 Park Avenue, New York, NY 10016.

Distributed in Australia by Capricorn Link (Australia) Pty. Ltd., P.O. Box 665, Lane Cove, New South Wales 2066, Australia.

British Library Cataloguing in Publication Data:
Katcher, Philip, 1941–
Union Forces of the American Civil War – (Soldiers fotofax)
1. American Civil War. Army operations by United States Army.
I. Title   II. Series
973.7'3
ISBN 0-85368-980-6

Line illustrations by the author.

Designed and edited by DAG Publications Ltd.
Designed by David Gibbons; layout by Cilla Eurich; typeset by Ronset Typesetters Ltd, Darwen, Lancashire, and Typesetters (Birmingham) Ltd, Warley, West Midlands; camerawork by M&E Reproductions, North Fambridge, Essex; printed and bound in Great Britain by The Alden Press, Oxford.

The American Civil War, which began when thirteen Southern states attempted to dissolve their bonds with the national government in late 1860-early 1861, was the most cataclysmic event in the history of the USA. More lives were changed, more soldiers and sailors put in the field, and more national institutions forever altered during the four years of that war than in any other period in American history.

This book cannot begin to cover the war in detail; it is intended, rather, to give the interested reader a look at the basics of those armed forces that fought to preserve the nation created by their grandfathers in 1776.

Photography had come into existence just over twenty years before the Civil War broke out. By 1861 photographers were to be found in every small town in America. Most of the two million of so soldiers and sailors had themselves photographed several times for family and friends. Many of these photographs have survived to provide historians with accurate data on uniforms and weapons.

While many men were photographed in dress uniform, a great number of photographs were taken in the field, where an enormous variety of dress – even civilian clothes – was to be seen.

US Army and Navy personnel of the period were not especially dressy; in fact, probably no war has seen less military-looking soldiers locked in combat. But the men were reasonably comfortable – or as comfortable as they could be in woollen uniforms in August in almost tropical weather – and the uniforms were convenient.

The basic US National military colour was blue. Soldiers generally wore dark-blue coats with, for dress, branch-of-service coloured piping, and sky-blue trousers (after December 1861), and dark-blue fatigue peaked caps or black, broad-brimmed dress hats. Officers wore much the same uniform, minus the piping. Sailors and officers in the Navy and Revenue Marine Cutter Service wore dark-blue dress that was very similar to that of the Royal Navy. Officers and men of the Marine Corps wore dark-blue fatigue caps or black dress shakos with dark-blue coats and sky-blue trousers with red trim.

Those were the regulation uniforms. There were, in addition, thousands of volunteers, wearing uniforms of virtually every imaginable colour. Grey was the most common colour among the volunteers, but these uniforms had largely disappeared from the front by 1862. Throughout the war, however, some regiments clung with pride to copies of zouave and chasseur uniforms often copied quite closely from those of the Imperial French Army.

Lasting four years and costing more casualties than all America's wars until Vietnam, the Civil War captured the public's interest to an extent unequalled by any other period in American history. Within the last two decades, tens of thousands of men and women have begun to attempt to recreate that period with authentically replicated uniforms, accoutrements, and weapons. Their efforts to bring the past to life are tremendous and it is to them that this book is dedicated.

Philip Katcher

▲4

▲5　▼6

4. Brigadier General Joseph Hooker wears the uniform of his rank with his buttons in pairs, black velvet collars and cuffs, and a single silver star in the centre of his shoulder-straps. His sword is the regulation field officer's model, similar to that worn by line officers but lighter in weight. Hooker commanded the Army of the Potomac at Chancellorsville in May 1863.

5. Major General Franz Sigel, a veteran of the 1848 insurrections in Germany, was one of the leaders of the American German community, from which a large number of Union soldiers was drawn. His uniform is a common field one, even for generals, including the fatigue blouse and white leather gloves. Sigel was a poor general and was removed from command after being beaten at New Market, Virginia in 1864.

6. Colonel Silas P. Richmond commanded the 3rd Massachusetts Infantry on its formation in the autumn of 1862. He wears the regulation uniform for his rank save for the broad-brimmed 'slouch hat' with its infantry insignia and regimental number worn as a cap badge. The 3rd served along the North Carolina coastline, being mustered out in June 1862. Richmond then commanded the 58th Massachusetts Infantry.

▲7

8▶

7. Uniforms that varied from regulations were common, even among high-ranking officers. Colonel William R. Lee, commander of the 20th Massachusetts Infantry, wears a single-breasted coat rather than the regulation double-breasted version. His cap has a plain infantry horn without a regimental number. The 20th left Massachusetts on 4 September 1861 and served in II Corps. Colonel Lee resigned in late 1862.

8. Colonel Thomas Cass, commander of the 9th Massachusetts Infantry, wears a loose frock-coat buttoned down the front with four brass buttons; white gloves, and white canvas and brown leather 'sporting shoes'. The latter were a common variation from issued shoes. Colonel Cass was mortally wounded near Richmond on 27 June 1862.

▲9 ▼10

▲11

9. Major D. T. Eranto, 89th New York Infantry, wears his regulation coat in a fashionable mode for the day, with only the top buttoned. The 89th, nicknamed 'The Dickinson Guard', served from 1861 to 1865. The regiment saw service along the North Carolina coast.

10. This unidentified officer was photographed in the most famous studio of the day, Brady's Photographic Studios, in either Washington, DC, or New York. His rank is indicated by an oak leaf in either gold (for a major) or silver (for a lieutenant colonel) on each side of his standing collar – quite against regulations, but not uncommon.

11. Captain Nathaniel Lyon, 2nd US Infantry, wears the regulation dress uniform of his rank; he is holding his dress cap. His sword is the regulation line officer's sword. Lyon was gazetted major general on 17 May 1861 and organized and led the Union forces that saved Missouri for the Union. He was killed in action at Wilson's Creek, Missouri on 10 August 1861.

12. A regulation company-grade officer, photographed in Sing Sing, New York, as he would have appeared on parade and in the field. His line officer's sword is hooked up with the hilt towards the rear, which was the preferred way of carrying it. The

star on his collar is, however, inexplicable.

13. First Lieutenant Levi Lincoln, Jr., 34th Massachusetts, has his small slouch hat on the table next to him. The 34th left Massachusetts on 15 August 1862 and served in the Shenandoah Valley until mustered out on 16 June 1865. Lieutenant Lincoln was photographed in Baltimore, probably at about the time he was demobilized.

▲14　▼15　　　　　▼16

14. These four company-grade officers of the 2nd Delaware Regiment give a good idea of the different types of hats and corps badges worn by officers of their grades. The two lieutenants second from left (Brady), and extreme right, wear their II Corps badges on the side of their slouch hats; First Lieutenant Thomas M. Wenie (far left), wears his on top of his kepi. Captain Charles H. Christmas has a plain, grey hat without cap badge.

15. This 6th New Jersey Infantry first lieutenant wears a commercially sold version of the III Corps badge on his left breast. It was made of silver, with the regimental number cut out of the diamond-shaped badge. Although this photograph was taken in late 1864 or early 1865, he still wears dark trousers (against regulations since 16 December 1861).

16. Assistant Surgeon William F. Reiber, 47th Pennsylvania Infantry, holds a non-regulation, eagle-headed sword that probably predates the Civil War by a number of years. It was not uncommon for officers to carry swords used by their fathers or grandfathers in earlier wars. Surgeon Reiber was mustered in on 30 October 1862 and resigned on 23 January 1865.

17. Captain DeWitt Clinton Lewis, 97th Pennsylvania Infantry, was photographed at about the time when he saved one of his men from drowning under fire at the battle of Secessionville, South Carolina, which act earned him the Medal of Honor. This award was given to four men of the 97th, the only regiment to be enlisted for three years in Pennsylvania's Chester County.

18. First Lieutenant James J. Skiles, 97th Pennsylvania

Infantry, was promoted from the ranks on 27 May 1863, and was wounded at Petersburg on 16 June 1864. He holds a foot officer's sword with a brass scabbard; most of these swords came with leather scabbards. His hat is an unusual one. The 97th was in X Corps in Florida, the Carolinas and around Richmond.

▲20 ▼21

▲19

19. First Lieutenant D. Divine, 143rd New York Infantry, was photographed in April 1864 in dark-blue trousers that had been against regulations for his rank for almost three years. The 143rd was part of VII Corps doing picket duty at White House Landing, Virginia, until reassigned to XI Corps on 14 July 1863.

20. The cap badge on this first lieutenant's dress cap (beside him) indicates membership of the 56th Pennsylvania Infantry. The regiment was mustered in on 1 September 1861 and fought at South Mountain, Fredericksburg, Chancellorsville and Brandy Station before being the first infantry regiment on the scene at Gettysburg in I Corps. There it lost 130 officers and men of the 252 who went into that battle.

21. Officers, such as this captain of the Veteran Reserve Corps, complained that the sky-blue coats with black velvet collars and cuffs became too easily soiled. By the war's end, VRC officers were allowed the same dark-blue coats as other officers wore. The VRC was considered an élite corps and was made up of veterans incapable of active service because of disease or wounds.

23▲   24▼

22. This man wears a regulation company-grade officer's coat without rank badges. His sword is the style worn by medical and pay department officers. His cap badge, however, is that of an enlisted infantryman. He wears white canvas and brown leather sporting shoes. This type of non-regulation dress was not at all uncommon.

23. Captain Harry Sleeper, 10th Massachusetts Artillery, wears the regulation shell jacket with gold Russian shoulder-knots of a light artillery officer. The 10th left Massachusetts on 2 October 1862, serving in the Army of the Potomac at Kelly's Ford, in the Wilderness, and Hatcher's Run. The last artillery round to be fired by II Corps and, with one exception, by the Army of the Potomac, came from the 10th. It was mustered out on 9 June 1865.

24. Company-grade officers often wore custom-made copies of the issue fatigue blouse. Captain G. Eland, for example, wore such a blouse with a black-lined collar that could be folded down for comfort. For more formal occasions, the blouse could be worn with the collar up to make a short dress coat.

22▲

▲25

25. This New York first lieutenant wears a custom-made four-button blouse with a breast pocket for a handkerchief. The blouse worn like this was very similar to the civilian day coat worn by businessmen of the period. The top of a military-style waistcoat with its standing collar can be seen just below his stiff, white shirt collar.

▲26

26. According to the 1861 dress regulations: 'Oficers are permitted to wear a plain dark-blue body-coat, with the button designating their respective corps, regiments, or departments, without any other mark or ornament upon it. Such a coat, however, is not to be considered as a dress for any military purpose.' Such is what this first lieutenant wears.

27▲　29▼

28▲

27. This medical cadet wears his rank insignia on his shoulders with a green stripe around his kepi which shows that he is in the Ambulance Corps of the Army of the Potomac or Army of the Cumberland. The short jacket was often worn in the field as a more comfortable alternative dress.

28. The three buttons and stripe around this first, or orderly sergeant's cuffs are not regulation (and cannot be explained), neither is the large stripe under his standing collar. However, the chevrons are perfectly regulation for that grade.

29. A number of non-regulation non-commissioned officer's chevrons appeared during the war, of which this is one example. This particular design was used by the commissary sergeant of the 20th Connecticut Infantry. The half-chevron on each cuff indicates three years' service. The frock coat is plain, without the regulation branch-of-service coloured piping.

▲30

▲31

30. A perfectly regulation 1861 infantry sergeant, photographed in Philadelphia, holding his forage cap. His non-commissioned officer's sword hangs from a frog on his waistbelt – many other non-commissioned officers preferred the shoulder-belt for the sword. Note the wide, sky-blue stripe down each trouser leg.

31. Massachusetts' soldiers, such as this sergeant, often appeared in dress frock-coats that differed from regulation in that the branch-of-service coloured piping on each cuff ran parallel to the sleeve bottom, not coming to a point on the front of the sleeve as per regulations. This sergeant does not wear the regulation trouser stripe. The company letter 'I' can be made out on his forage cap top.

32. Most chevrons were made by sewing stripes of cloth on a dark-blue background and then sewing the background to the sleeves. This Maryland sergeant wears chevrons made from one large piece of sky-blue cloth with dark-blue lines chain-stitched at parallel intervals to give the same effect. In some cases, stripes of branch-of-service colour were sewn directly on to the sleeves themselves.

33. This West Chester, Pennsylvania corporal wears service chevrons on each cuff which indicates war-time service. They are sky-blue edged with red. His cap apparently bears the letters 'PVV', probably standing for Pennsylvania Veteran Volunteer. The sky-blue military-style waistcoat he wears was not issued, but most men liked to wear them and had them sent from home.

34. In 1861 Connecticut issued its first regiments with locally made frock-coats without regulation branch-of-service colour piping. This New Haven corporal wears one of them. These early uniforms were made of cheap, rough cloth which wore out very quickly. The 1st Connecticut returned from the First Bull Run, after three months' service, in trousers made from old blankets, captured Confederate zouave dress, and various rags.

▲35 ▼36

▲37

35. Musicians wore their dress uniform coats or jackets with an additional adornment. It included branch-of-service coloured piping from each coat button, edged by the same piping, 'the whole presenting something of what is called the herring-bone form . . .' This infantry musician also wears the dress brass shoulder-scales demanded by regulations.

36. According to regulations, the dress hat, as worn here by the private on the left, was to be 'looped up on the left side' in the infantry and artillery, and on the other side for all other branches of service. Feathers were to be worn on the opposite side. In practice, these hat brims were worn hooked up on either side, it not being clear whether the left side as worn or as seen was meant.

37. Soldiers usually had a choice of taking their dress-frock coat or fatigue blouse into the field with them. In the Army of the Potomac, some 46 per cent wore their dress coats instead of fatigue blouses.

38▲　39▶

Private George M. Stevens, 9th
New Hampshire Infantry, as was
true of the majority of New
Hampshire men, preferred the
dress coat. Stevens is armed
with an M1841 rifle, the
'Mississippi Rifle'.

38. Private Harry Gordrick
shows how the foot soldier's
dress coat could be worn as a
civilian-style outfit, with its
standing collar folded down. He
wears only seven buttons on his
dark-blue waistcoat with its
standing collar; most of these
waiscoats had nine buttons.

39. The type of red-trimmed
zouave jacket worn by this
sergeant of the 95th
Pennsylvania Infantry,
nicknamed 'Gosline's Zouaves',
was also worn by soldiers in the
69th Pennsylvania Infantry
(with green trim) and 72nd
Pennsylvania Infantry (with red
trim). This sergeant wears the
VI Corps badge on his waistcoat.
The 95th mustered in during
October 1861 and served in the
Army of the Potomac until its
demobilization on 17 June
1865.

40. The 95th Pennsylvania Infantry's zouave jacket was not worn over an issue waistcoat, although some of the men acquired waistcoats to wear with their jackets. Often, therefore, the men wore fancy shirts, such as this man's which buttons all the way down the front with brass ball buttons like that worn on the jacket.

41. Some eight per cent of the Army of the Potomac's infantrymen wore waist-length jackets in the field. Many were cut such as the one worn by the regimental quartermaster sergeant. His jacket has state-issue buttons but is made without trim. He carried the non-commissioned officer's sword and has veteran stripes on each cuff.

42. For dress, mounted enlisted men, such as this light artilleryman, wore uniform jackets trimmed with branch-of-service coloured piping around the collar, cuffs, front and bottom, and back seams. Volunteers preferred a lower collar and often had their jacket collars cut down with only a single buttonhole of lace on each side.

43 ▲   44 ▼

45 ▲

43. The mounted man's regulation dress jacket had two buttons and false buttonholes made from branch-of-service coloured piping, as worn by this man. In the field many mounted men, too, preferred the broad-brimmed slouch hats to issue peaked caps. This man also appears to wear the issue grey flannel shirt, which was cut pullover fashion.

44. Corporal Windsor B. Smith, 1st Maine Cavalry, wears the mounted man's dress jacket with only the top two buttons fastened, a common practice. Smith joined the regiment's Company 'K' in September 1862; was promoted to corporal on 1 July 1863; was captured around Petersburg on 29 September 1864; was exchanged April 1865; and was discharged on 24 July 1865.

45. This oddly trimmed jacket and large cap badge was worn by members of the 8th Pennsylvania Cavalry. The unit was raised as mounted rifles in mid-1861 and served with the Army of the Potomac. In the advance at Chancellorsville, performing a hopeless charge against Jackson's flanking force, the unit lost 150 men. The 8th served in 135 battles, a record equalled by only one other command in the Union Army. It was mustered out on 11 August 1865.

CHRONOLOGY

Note that some battles were given different names by the opposing sides. What the Confederates called Sharpsburg, the Union forces called Antietam. Union names have been used in this list.

1860
6 November: Abraham Lincoln elected US President.

1861
13 March: Army dress regulations issued.

12–13 April: Siege of Fort Sumter, South Carolina (CS victory).

15 April: President calls for 75,000 volunteers to put down the rebellion.

19 April: Blockade of Southern ports declared.

9 May: US Naval Academy moved to Newport, Rhode Island.

9 June: US Sanitary Commission formed for soldier relief.

21 July: First Battle of Bull Run (CS victory).

9 August: Army orders 10,000 *chasseurs à pied* (light infantry) uniforms from M. Alexis Godillot of Paris.

10 August: All Army mounted units made cavalry regiments, numbered 1 to 6.

12–13 September: Battle of Cheat Mountain, Virginia (US victory).

7 November: Capture of Port Royal, South Carolina.

14 November: US Christian Commission for soldier relief formed in New York City.

21 November: Army chaplains authorized plain black frock-coats, trousers and hat.

25 November: Army officers authorized use of enlisted mounted men's overcoats in the field.

16 December: Sky-blue trousers made Army-wide regulation to replace dark-blue trousers.

1862
6–16 February: Forts Henry and Donelson captured (US victory).

6–8 March: Battle of Pea Ridge, Arkansas (US victory).

8 March: Army of Potomac divided into five Corps.

9 March: USS *Monitor* stands off CSS *Virginia* (US victory).

14 March: Capture of New Bern, North Carolina.

28 March: Battle of Glorieta Pass, New Mexico (US victory).

5 April to 2 July: Peninsula campaign against Richmond (CS victory).

6–7 April: Battle of Shiloh, Tennessee (US victory).

7 April: Island No. 10 captured.

16 April: Slaves in District of Columbia freed.

29 April: New Orleans occupied.

10 May: Norfolk, Virginia occupied.

5 June: Army Hospital Corps authorized.

18 June: Double-breasted jacket with two rows of six medium-sized buttons authorized for Navy leading petty officers.

1 July: First national income tax authorized.

2 July: Government calls for 300,000 volunteers for three years' service.

16 July: Navy ranks of rear admiral, commodore, lieutenant commander, and ensign created; new insignia authorized.

4 August: Draft of 300,000 men ordered by Secretary of War.

26–27 August: Second Battle of Bull Run (CS victory).

18 August: Indian uprising in Minnesota.

17 September: Battle of Antietam (draw, but an effective US victory).

23 September: Emancipation Proclamation frees slaves in revolting states, effective 1 January 1863.

8 October: Battle of Perryville (US victory).

November: First black regiments formed.

13 December: Battle of Fredericksburg (CS victory).

31 December to 2 January: Battle of Murfreesboro (US victory).

1863
26 January: Recruiting of blacks in Massachusetts authorized.

28 February: USS *Montauk* destroys CSS *Nashville*.

3 March: Writ of Habeas Corpus suspended, conscription measure passed; Army Signal Corps created.

21 March: Badges for different Army of Potomac Corps ordered.

28 April: Invalid Corps, later Veteran Reserve Corps, created.

1–3 May: Battle of Chancellorsville (CS victory).

14 May: Jackson, Mississippi captured.

16 May: Battle of Champion's Hill (US victory).

23 May: Navy authorizes new officer insignia using narrow gold stripes; line officers to wear a star over the stripes.

25 June: Veteran Volunteers, men with three years' service, authorized service half-chevrons.

1–3 July: Battle of Gettysburg (US victory).

4 July: Vicksburg captured, River Mississippi in US hands.

13–14 July: New York draft riots.

1 September: Little Rock, Arkansas captured.

4 September: Knoxville, Tennessee captured.

19–20 September: Battle of Chickamauga (CS victory).

27 October to 7 November: First Sanitary Fair held to benefit Sanitary Commission in Chicago.

6 November: Brownsville, Texas captured.

19 November: Lincoln delivers Gettysburg Address.

25 November: Lookout Mountain overrun, Chattanooga freed.

8 December: Pardons promised for surrendering CS officials.

1864
6 January: Canyon de Chelly Campaign against Navajos in New Mexico, ends in Indian defeat.

11 March: Army Ambulance Corps created by Congress.

3 May: Wilderness campaign begins; fighting in Virginia will not end until Lee surrenders.

13 May: Battle of Resaca, first major battle in Atlanta campaign.

8 June: Lincoln nominated for second term.

19 June: USS *Kearsage* sinks CSS *Albama* off French coast.

11 July: Southern raid on Washington defeated.

22 July: Battle of Atlanta (US victory).

5 August: CSS *Tennessee* captured.

20 August: Revenue Cutter Service officers receive ½inch gold stripes for rank insignia.

25 August: Army chaplains authorized black braid herringbone design on their frock-coats.

29 August: Democrats nominate George B. McClellan for president.

1 September: Confederates abandon Atlanta.

19 September: Battle of Winchester, Virginia (US victory).

7 October: USS *Wachusett* sinks CSS *Florida* off Brazil.

19 October: Battle of Cedar Creek, Virginia; Shenandoah Valley secured.

19 October: Confederates in Canada raid St. Albans, Vermont, in the most northerly action of the war.

8 November: Abraham Lincoln re-elected to presidency.

16 November: Sherman begins march from Atlanta to
Savannah on the Georgia coast.
28 November: Veteran Volunteer Corps, made up of discharged
veterans, authorized; was never fully organized.
29 November: Colorado cavalry massacres peaceful Cheyennes
at Sand Creek, Colorado.
15–16 December: Battle of Nashville; Southern Army of
Tennessee destroyed.
20 December: Confederates abandon Savannah, Georgia.
21 December: Navy rank of vice admiral created; David
Farragut named first to hold the rank.

1865
14 January: Navy authorized sack coats for officers.
15 January: Fort Fisher, last Southern port, falls.
3 February: Unsuccessful peace conference at Hampton Roads,
Virginia.
17 February: Columbia, capital of South Carolina, captured.
18 February: Charleston, South Carolina, where war began,
captured.
4 March: Lincoln inaugurated to second term.
21 March: Battle of Bentonville, North Carolina, last major
battle of the war (US victory).
1 April: Battle of Five Forks, Virginia (US victory).
3 April: Richmond, Virginia, Southern capital, captured.
4 April: Lincoln visits Richmond.
9 April: Army of Northern Virginia surrenders to the Army of the
Potomac.
12 April: Mobile, Alabama, last major Southern city in
Confederate hands, captured.
14 April: Lincoln shot by actor John Wilkes Booth.
26 April: Joseph Johnston's army surrenders.
26 May: Trans-Mississippi Command surrenders.
6 November: CSS *Shenandoah* surrenders to British
authorities.

CORPS OF THE US ARMY

Each corps contained at least three divisions; each division,
three brigades; each brigade, usually five regiments; each
regiment, ten companies; each company, 100 men.

I Corps: Formed in the Mountain Department 12 August 1862;
discontinued 23 March 1864; reorganized 28 November 1864.
II Corps: Formed in the Shenandoah Department 12 August
1862; redesignated XI Corps 12 September 1862 while new II
Corps formed in the Army of the Potomac on that date;
discontinued 28 June 1865.
III Corps: Formed in the District of Washington 12 August
1862; redesignated XII Corps 12 September 1862 while new III
Corps formed in Army of the Potomac on that date;
discontinued 23 March 1864.
IV Corps: Formed in Army of the Potomac 12 September 1862;
discontinued 1 August 1863; reformed from XX and XXI Corps
28 September 1863; discontinued 1 August 1865.
V Corps: Formed in Army of the Potomac 22 July 1862;
discontinued 28 June 1865.
VI Corps: Formed in Army of the Potomac 22 July 1862,
discontinued 28 June 1865.
VII Corps: Formed of troops under General Dix's command 22
July 1862; troops transferred to XVIII Corps 1 August 1863;

reformed in Department of Arkansas 6 January 1864;
discontinued 1 August 1865.
VIII Corps: Formed of troops under General Wool's command 22
July 1862; discontinued 1 August 1865.
IX Corps: Formed in Department of North Carolina 22 July
1862; discontinued 27 July 1865.
X Corps: Formed in Department of South 3 September 1862;
discontinued 3 December 1864; reformed in North Carolina 27
March 1865; discontinued 1 August 1865.
XI Corps: Formed in Shenandoah Department 12 September
1862; consolidated with XII Corps to form XX Corps 4 April
1864.
XII Corps: Formed of troops under General McDowell 12
September 1862; consolidated with XI Corps to form XX Corps
4 April 1864.
XIII Corps: Formed in Department of Tennessee 24 October
1862; discontinued 11 June 1864; reformed 18 February
1865; discontinued 20 July 1865.
XIV Corps: Formed in Department of the Cumberland 24
October 1862; discontinued 1 August 1865.
XV Corps: Formed of troops under General Grant 18 December
1862; discontinued 1 August 1865.
XVI Corps: Formed of troops under General Grant 18 December
1862; discontinued 7 November 1864; reformed 18 February
1865; discontinued 20 July 1865.
XVII Corps: Formed of troops under General Grant 18 December
1862; discontinued 1 August 1865.
XVIII Corps: Formed in North Carolina 24 December 1862;
designated to include troops from North Carolina and Virginia
in the Army of the Potomac 17 July 1864; discontinued 3
December 1864.
XIX Corps: Formed in Department of the Gulf 5 January 1863;
discontinued in West Mississippi 7 November 1864;
discontinued 20 March 1865.
XX Corps: Formed in Army of the Cumberland 9 January 1863;
consolidated with XXI Corps to form IV Corps 28 September
1863; reformed from XI and XII Corps 4 April 1864;
discontinued 1 June 1865.
XXI Corps: Formed in Army of the Cumberland 9 January 1863;
consolidated with XX Corps to form IV Corps 28 September
1863.
XXII Corps: Formed in Department of Washington 2 February
1863.
XXIII Corps: Formed in Kentucky 27 April 1863; discontinued 1
August 1865.
XXIV Corps: Formed from white troops of X and XVIII Corps 3
December 1864; discontinued 1 August 1865.
XXV Corps: Formed of coloured troops from Department of
Virginia and North Carolina 3 December 1864; discontinued 8
January 1866.
Cavalry Corps, Army of the Potomac: Formed 15 April 1863.

SQUADRONS OF THE US NAVY

North Atlantic Squadron: Formed to blockade the Virginia and
North Carolina coasts.
South Atlantic Squadron: Formed to blockade the Atlantic coast
from North Carolina to Cape Florida.
East Gulf Squadron: Formed 21 February 1862 to blockade the
southern and western Florida peninsula.

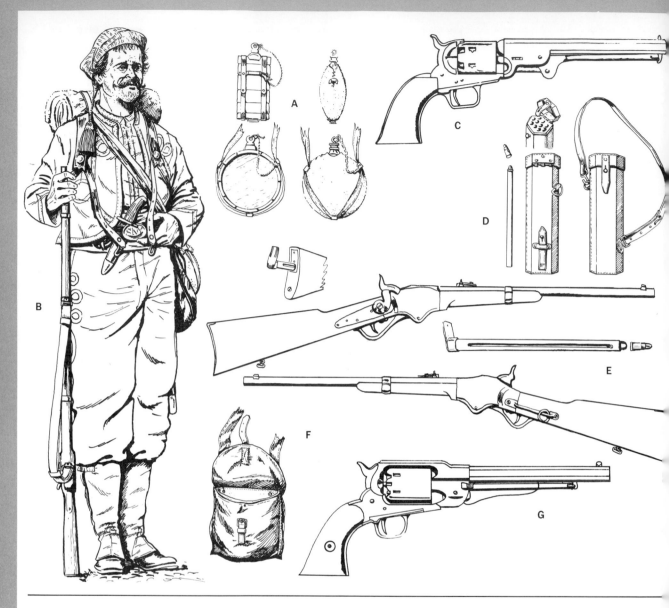

A: The Model 1858 canteen was an oblate spheroid tin canteen covered with grey, brown or blue wool, and suspended by a white cotton sling. A maker's name usually appeared on the pewter spout into which was placed a cork with an iron ring keeper. This canteen replaced earlier tin drum style, india rubber, leather, and wood canteens, such as the one to the left of the M1858 model, as the standard canteen some years before the war. Some wood canteens such as seen here saw limited, militia use by Union forces.

B: This private in the 9th New York Volunteer Infantry Regiment wears a typical Union Army copy of French zouave dress. The plain felt fez was red with a blue tassel; the jacket, waistcoat and trousers were all dark-blue trimmed in magenta; the sash was magenta; and the leggings were white. Red trousers were more typical, especially among zouave units that had imported French-made uniforms. The 9th was formed in April 1861, serving at Roanoke Island, North Carolina; Antietam; and Fredericksburg, before being mustered out in May 1863.

C: The Colt 0.36 calibre 'Navy' revolver was the handgun of choice of most Army and Navy officers as well as being a standard issue pistol in all services. A handsome weapon, it had walnut grips, a brass trigger guard, and blued steel barrel, frame, and cylinder.

D: The patented Blakeslee Quickloader cartridge box was designed for use with the Spencer carbine. It was slung over the right shoulder to the left front side, hooking on the waistbelt.

E: Almost 95,000 Spencer carbines were acquired by the Army for cavalry use. The weapon was very advanced for its time, using fixed, brass cartridge ammunition that loaded into tubes, inserted into the weapon's butt, to allow the firing of seven shots before being reloaded. A rifle version also saw limited use by Union infantry.

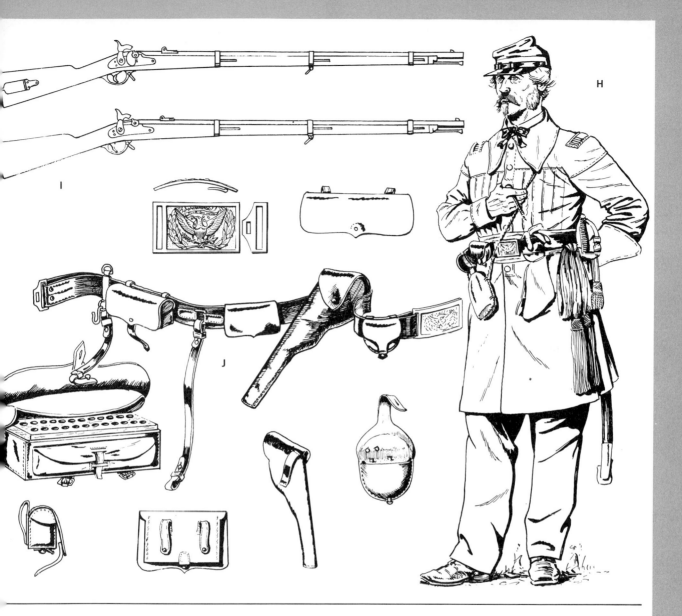

F: The issue haversack was designed to hold rations and, during campaigns, extra ammunition. It was waterproofed by being painted with a black, tar-like coating. A separate white food bag was held inside by means of three buttons, one on the front and two on the back. The food bags were often cut up for use as gun cleaning patches.

G: The Remington revolver came in Army (0.44) and Navy (0.36) calibres and was very popular because of the backstrap over the top of the cylinder which made it a stronger weapon than the Colt. A slight variation of the original Model 1861 version appeared in 1863, but both weapons looked very much alike.

H: Until June 1862 Rhode Island produced a state uniform for its two infantry regiments that included a dark-blue forage cap, a dark-blue hunting shirt and grey trousers. This captain wears the single-breasted version; a double-breasted version was worn by majors and above. His flask is a silver one, privately purchased.

I: The main infantry longarm was the Model 1855 rifled musket, seen left, and variations thereof. The M1855 featured an elaborate sight, a patchbox, and a patented automatic priming system which used percussion caps on a waterproofed roll of paper that was advanced with each cock. In 1861 a cheaper version of the M1855 appeared (seen on right). It eliminated the patch box and primer and included a three-leaf sight. Other versions appeared in 1863 and 1864 without the cleanout screw below the nipple and with an improved hammer.

J: The cavalryman's equipment included a sword belt with a brass belt-plate that bore the national eagle design within a silver wreath. The equipment on the waistbelt (not shown to proportion), included a leather pouch for percussion caps with a lamb's fleece that retained the caps; a holster (a privately purchased officer's model seen here), a small pouch for pistol ammunition; and a large pouch for carbine ammunition.

West Gulf Squadron: Formed 21 February 1862 to blockade from Pensacola to the Mexican border.
Mississippi Squadron: Formed to open and maintain free traffic on the River Mississippi.

Pacific Squadron: Formed to maintain the freedom of the high seas for American shipping in the Pacific Ocean.
West India Squadron: Formed to convoy California steamers; discontinued 3 October 1864.

THE US ARMED FORCES IN STATISTICS

Combat Units of the US Army

Cavalry Regiments	258
Independent Cavalry Companies	170
Artillery Regiments	57
Independent Artillery Companies	22
Independent Artillery Batteries	232
Infantry Regiments	1,666
Independent Infantry Companies	306

Strength of the US Army

1 January 1861	16,367
1 July 1861	186,751
1 January 1862	575,917
31 March 1862	637,126
1 January 1863	918,191
1 January 1864	860,737
1 January 1865	959,460
1 May 1865	1,000,516

Losses in the US Army

Killed	61,362
Died of wounds	34,773
Died of disease	183,287
Accidentally killed	306
Executed by sentence	267
Missing in action	6,749
Honourably discharged	174,577
Discharged for disability	224,306
Dishonourably discharged	2,693
Dismissed	2,423
Cashiered	274
Resigned	22,281
Deserted	199,045
Total casualties	912,343

Top Ten Fighting Regiments
(as indicated by total losses)

Regiment	Corps	Percentage Losses
2nd Wisconsin Infantry	I	19.7
1st Maine Heavy Artillery	II	19.2
57th Massachusetts Infantry	IX	19.1
140th Pennsylvania Infantry	II	17.4
26th Wisconsin Infantry	XI	17.2
7th Wisconsin Infantry	I	17.2
69th New York Infantry	II	17.1
40th Pennsylvania Infantry	V	16.6
142nd Pennsylvania Infantry	I	16.5
141st Pennsylvania Infantry	III	16.1

SHIPS OF THE US NAVY

Date	Ships	No. Guns	Tonnage
March 1861	69	1,346	unknown
December 1861	264	2,557	218,016
December 1862	427	3,268	340,036
December 1863	588	4,443	467,967
December 1864	671	4,610	510,396

WEAPONS OF THE US ARMED FORCES

FIELD ARTILLERY

M1857 Gun Howitzer (Napoleon): Adopted 1857. Smoothbore. Tube, bronze, 1,227 pounds, 66 inches long. Shot, 12.3 pounds. Charge, 2.5 pounds. Muzzle velocity, 1,440fps. Range at 3° elevation, 1,619 yards. 1,127 produced. A preferred anti-personnel weapon.

10-pound Parrott: Adopted 1860. Rifled. Tube, iron, 74 inches long. Shot, 9.5 pounds. Charge, 1.0 pound. Muzzle velocity, 1,230fps. Range at 3° elevation, 1,850 yards. 587 produced. Accurate at long range, especially for counter-battery work.

3-inch Ordnance Rifle (Rodman): Adopted 1861. Rifled. Tube, iron, 69 inches long. Shot, 9.5 pounds. Charge, 1 pound. Muzzle velocity, 1,215fps. Range at 3° elevation, 1,830 yards. 925 produced. Used much as were the Parrott guns.

INFANTRY LONGARMS

M1841 Rifle (Mississippi): 0.54 calibre, rifled, 52.66 inches long, 33-inch barrel, browned barrel, brass furniture. 25,296 produced. A common early war weapon, taking a sabre bayonet.

M1842 Musket: 0.69 calibre, smoothbore, 57.75 inches long. 42-inch barrel, bright finished iron furniture, 279,501 produced. Although obsolete, often used by militia.

M1855 Rifled Musket: 0.58 calibre, rifled, 56 inches long, 40-inch barrel, polished iron furniture, 39,792 produced. An excellent weapon, although the patented Maynard primer and elaborate sight made it too expensive for mass production.

M1861 Rifled Musket: Dimensions as above, 670,617 acquired by the Army. Essentially a simplified M1855 with a three-blade sight and plain nipple. Further variations were made in 1863, first by flattening the nipple bolster and removing the barrel band springs, then by replacing the springs. Many of these weapons were made by private contractors who also sold them to state militias.

P1853 Rifled Muskets: 0.577 calibre, rifled, 55 inches long, 3-inch barrel, bright finish iron with brass nosecap and buttplate and trigger guard. 428,292 acquired by the Army. The regulation British Army longarm of the period, these were the second most popular US Army longarm of the period.

M1854 Lorenz Rifled Musket: 0.54 calibre, rifled, 52.75 inches long, bright finish iron. 226,294 acquired by the Army. Made in Austria and lacking the quality of British- or American-made arms, many soldiers still thought highly of their light-weight Lorenz rifled muskets.

M1861 Whitney Naval Rifle (Plymouth): 0.69 calibre, rifled, 50 inches long, bright barrel and blued steel furniture and lock. The standard Navy-issue rifle, it came with a short-bladed Dahlgren knife bayonet.

CARBINES

Burnside: 0.54 calibre, rifled, 40 inches long, breechloading. 55,567 acquired by the Army. Four models, differing only slightly in appearance, of this weapon designed by Major General Ambrose Burnside, were used during the war. It used a special brass cartridge.

M1859 Sharps: 0.52 calibre, rifled, 37.75 inches long, breechloading. 80,512 acquired by the Army. The Sharps, which fired a paper-wrapped combustible cartridge, was one of the most popular carbines of the war.

Smith: 0.50 calibre, rifled, 39.5 inches long, breechloading. 30,062 acquired by the Army. The Smith broke open in the middle like a shotgun, using a rubber cartridge to prevent flash at the breech.

Spencer: 0.52 calibre, rifled, 39 inches long, magazine-fed. 94, 196 acquired by the Army. The Spencer used a tube magazine that held seven brass cartridges; the most technically advanced longarm of the period (save possibly for the Henry which saw little action) as well as the most popular carbine.

Starr: 0.54 calibre, rifled, 37.5 inches long, breechloading. 25,603 acquired by the Army. The Starr was very much like the Sharps carbine, in action as well as appearance.

REVOLVERS

M1860 Colt Army: 0.44 calibre, 14 inches long, 129,730 acquired by Army. The standard cavalry pistol.

M1851 Colt Navy: 0.36 calibre, 13 inches long, 17,010 acquired by Army. Preferred by officers, and was the issue Navy weapon.

M1861 Remington: Came in both 0.44 calibre Army and 0.36 Navy versions, 13.75 inches long (Army version). 125,314 Army and 1,901 Navy versions acquired by Army. The backstrap across its cylinder made this a more rugged weapon than the Colt.

EDGED WEAPONS

M1840 Heavy Cavalry Sabre: 41.5 inches long, brass hilt with leather-wrapped wooden grips, blade 1.25 inches wide at hilt, iron scabbard, 189,114 acquired by the Army.

M8160 Light Cavalry Sabre: 41 inches long, same as above but lighter, blade 1 inch wide at hilt, 203,285 acquired by the Army.

M1840 Light Artillery Sabre: 37–38 inches long, single brass guard and leather-wrapped grips, blade 1.25 inches wide at hilt, iron scabbard, 20,757 acquired by Army.

M1833 Foot Artillery Sword: 25.25 inches long, all brass hilt, blade 1.75 inches wide at hilt, leather scabbard, 2,152 acquired by the Army. A copy of the Roman thrusting sword.

M1840 Non-Commissioned Officer's Sword: 38 inches long, all brass hilt, blade 0.875 inches wide at hilt, leather or iron scabbard, 86,655 acquired by the Army.

M1840 Musician's Sword: 34 inches long and lacking counterguards but otherwise a close copy of the NCO's sword, 33,531 acquired by the Army.

Officers' Swords: Cavalry and light artillery officers wore basically the same sword as did their men, with additional engraving. Foot officers carried the M1850 sword with an ornate guard and fishskin-wrapped grips in leather or brass scabbards. Medical and Pay Department officers had a special all-brass (except the blade) straight sword for dress occasions. The M1850 General and Field Officer's sword was quite like the foot officer's sword, but lighter. However, the M1860 sword for these officers was a straight sword in a metal scabbard with a quite ornate guard.

UNIFORMS OF THE FEDERAL FORCES

Army and Marine Corps/Navy Commissioned Officers' Insignia
(Worn on shoulder-straps, edged in gold, the insignia on branch-of-service coloured cloth for the Army; on black shoulder-straps, edged in gold with silver branch-of-service devices in the centre for the Navy; and on Russian shoulder-knots for the Marine Corps and Army Light Artillery.)

Major General/Rear Admiral: two silver stars.
Brigadier General/Commodore: one silver star.
Colonel/Captain: a silver spread eagle, having in the right talon an olive branch and in the left a bundle of arrows, an escutcheon on the breast (Navy on an anchor).
Lieutenant Colonel/Commander: a silver leaf at each end of the strap.
Major/Lieutenant Commander: a gold leaf at each end of the strap.
Captain/Lieutenant: two gold bars at each end of the strap.
First Lieutenant/Master: a gold bar at each end of the strap.
Second Lieutenant/Ensign: A plain strap.
Medical cadet (Army only): a 3-inch-long gold stripe, on top of a wider green stripe.

Army and Marine Corps Enlisted Men's Sleeve Insignia
(Chevrons worn above the elbow in branch-of-service colours for Army, points down; in yellow edged with red, points up, for Marines.)

Sergeant Major: three chevrons and an arc in silk.
Quartermaster Sergeant: three chevrons and a tie in silk.
Company Quartermaster Sergeant (Army only, after 1862): three chevrons and a single tie.
Ordnance Sergeant (Army only): three chevrons and a star in crimson silk.
Hospital Steward (Army only): an emerald-green half-chevron edged with yellow silk; a yellow caduceus in the centre.
First Sergeant: three chevrons and a lozenge in worsted.
Sergeant: three chevrons in worsted.
Corporal: two chevrons in worsted.
Pioneer (Army only): two crossed hatchets in branch of service colour.
Signal Corpsman (Army only): crossed signal flags, red and white (after 22 August 1864).
Ambulance Corpsman (Army only): green half-chevron (after August 1862 in Army of the Potomac, January 1864 in Army of the Cumberland, red in XVIII Corps.
Hospital Corpsman (Army only): green half-chevron (After 5 June 1862).

Army Branch-of-Service Colours
Artillery: scarlet.
Cavalry: yellow.
Engineers: yellow.
Infantry: sky-blue.
Medical: crimson (officers' shoulder-straps, black; hospital stewards' hat cords, mixed buff and green).
Ordnance: crimson.
Staff (officers only): black.

Army Cap Badges
(Embroidered on a black velvet background for officers, stamped brass for enlisted men.)

General and Staff Officers: silver Old English letters 'US' within a gold wreath.

Corps of Engineers: turreted castle (silver within a gold wreath for officers, brass for men).

Topographical Engineers: gold shield within a gold wreath.

Ordnance Department: gold flaming bomb.

Cavalry: crossed sabres, number of the regiment at the cross of the sabres (also brass Company letter for men).

Artillery: crossed cannon, the number of the regiment above the intersection of the cannon (also Company letter for men).

Infantry: a bugle, the regimental number inside the horn loop (under a Company letter for enlisted men).

Hospital Steward: white Roman letters 'US' within a brass wreath.

Signal Corps: crossed red-and-white signal flags under a silver torch and letters 'US' within a gold wreath (officers only; after 22 August 1864).

Sharpshooters: crossed rifles under Old English letters 'US' and over letters 'SS'.

Veteran Volunteers: seven-pointed star (after 18 June 1865).

Sashes

Generals: buff silk.
Other Army and Marine officers: crimson silk.
Army Medical Department: emerald-green silk.
Army and Marine First Sergeants and above: red worsted.

Army Corps Badges

Army corps badges were made from cloth or painted metal and worn on the hat top or side or left breast. They were first adopted in the Army of the Potomac on 21 March 1863. They were red for the corps' first division, white for its second, and blue for its third.

I Corps: a circle.
II Corps: a cloverleaf.
III Corps: a diamond.
IV Corps: a triangle.
V Corps: a Maltese cross.
VI Corps: a Greek cross (green for the 1863 Light Division).
VII Corps: a five-pointed star within a crescent.
VIII Corps: a six-pointed star.
IX Corps: a crossed cannon and anchor on a shield (green for the fourth division).
X Corps: the outline of a four-sided fort.
XI Corps: a crescent.
XII Corps: a five-pointed star.
XIII Corps: no badge adopted.
XIV Corps: an acorn.
XV Corps: a cartridge box with the motto '40 rounds' on a diamond.
XVI Corps: a circle with four bullets, the points toward the centre cut out of it.
XVII Corps: an arrow.
XVIII Corps: a cross with foliate sides.
XIX Corps: a four-pointed star.
XX Corps: a five-pointed star (green for fourth division).
XXI Corps: no badge adopted.
XXII Corps: a quinquefoliate shape.
XXIII Corps: a shield.
XXIV Corps: a heart.
XXV Corps: a square.

Army Zouave and Chasseur Regiments

The following regiments wore a variation of French zouave or chasseur dress at some time during their services.

Zouave Regiments: 11th Indiana, 33rd New Jersey, 35th New Jersey, 3rd New York, 5th New York, 9th New York, 10th New York, 11th New York, 17th New York, 44th New York, 53rd New York, 62nd New York, 74th New York, 140th New York, 146th New York, 164th New York, 165th New York, 34th Ohio, 23rd Pennsylvania, 72nd Pennsylvania, 76th Pennsylvania, 91st Pennsylvania, 95th Pennsylvania, 114th Pennsylvania, 155th Pennsylvania.

Chasseur Regiments: 18th Massachusetts, 12th New York State Militia, 49th New York, 72nd New York, 83rd Pennsylvania.

Navy Equivalent Rank

There were two grades of Navy officer, executive (deck) and civil. Each grade of civil officer had a unique title; they wore basically the same dress as equivalent executive officers with a special branch device on their shoulder-straps and minus the executive star over their cuff lace.

Commodore: Chief of the Bureaux of Medicine and Surgery, Provisions and Clothing, Steam Engineering, Construction.

Caption: Fleet Surgeon, Paymaster, or Engineer; Surgeon, Paymaster or Chief Engineer more than 15 years' service; Naval Constructor more than 20 years' service.

Commander: Surgeon, Paymaster, or Chief Engineer more than 5 years' service; Naval Constructor, Chaplain, or Professor of Mathematics more than 12 years' service.

Lieutenant Commander: Surgeon, Paymaster, or Chief Engineer less than 5 years' service; Naval Constructor, Chaplain, or Professor of Mathematics less than 12 years' service.

Lieutenant: Passed Assistant Surgeon.

Master: Assistant Surgeon, Paymaster, or Naval Constructor; First Assistant Engineer, Secretary.

Engine: Second Assistant Engineer.

Midshipman; Third Assistant Engineer; Clerk.

Naval Officers' Cuff Lace Insignia

Bars of gold lace worn on each cuff to indicate rank. A star was worn by executive officers in 1862 and by all deck officers after May 1863.

	1852	June 1862	May 1863
Rear Admiral	None	3 broad, 3 narrow bars	8 bars
Commodore	None	3 broad, 2 narrow bars	7 bars
Captain	3 broad	3 broad bars	6 bars
Commander	2 broad	2 broad, 1 narrow bars	5 bars
Lieutenant Commander	none	2 broad bars	4 bars
Lieutenant	1 broad	1 broad, 1 narrow bar	3 bars
Master	3 buttons	1 broad bar	2 bars
Ensign	None	1 narrow bar	1 bar

Revenue Marine Cutter Service Commissioned Officers' Insignia
(On blue shoulder-straps edged with gold.)

Captain: two crossed fouled anchors.
First Lieutenant: one fouled anchor over a shield in the centre with two gold bars at each end.

Second Lieutenant: one fouled anchor over a shield in the centre with one gold bar at each end.
Third Lieutenant: one fouled anchor over a shield.
Chief Engineer: an anchor over a gold wheel.
First Assistant Engineer: a gold wheel.
Second Assistant Engineer: a plain strap.

Revenue Marine Cutter Service Officers' Cuff Lace Insignia

Regulations in force at the start of the War had been written in 1843 and called for black cuff lace. This was changed to gold in 1862 and new regulations in August 1863 called for a gold Treasury Department shield over the top lace bar for all deck officers.

	1843	1862	1863
Captain	1 broad bar	2 bars	4 bars
First Lieutenant	3 buttons	1 bar	3 bars
Second Lieutenant	3 buttons	1 bar	2 bars
Third Lieutenant	plain cuffs	1 bar	1 bar

47▲

46. This cavalryman wears a plain uniform jacket (uniform jackets came to a point in front; shell jackets were cut straight around). This was a common type of mounted man's jacket; his has a left breast pocket. He carries a revolver in a holster on his right hip, and his sabre hangs from his left. A black leather pouch worn on the left front hip contains his copper percussion caps.

47. Eli Nichols wears the regulation uniform of a private in Company 'K', 9th Veteran Reserve Corps Regiment. The jacket is cut like a slightly longer version of the mounted man's jacket, in sky-blue with dark-blue trim. The 9th was part of the force that defended Washington against Jubal Early's attack in 1864 until VI Corps could arrive to relieve them. Nichols served in the 114th New York Infantry before being transferred to the VRC.

48. Since they were in permanent posts, VRC members sometimes purchased uniforms that were better made than issue ones. This private of the 13th VRC, stationed in the Boston area, wears a custommade jacket whose trim is lighter than usual, and a kepi with his regimental cap badge.

49. New York issued its troops with a special uniform, consisting of a dark-blue, waistlength jacket with sky-blue trim around its standing collar and epaulettes. The 16th New York Infantry also received broadbrimmed straw hats in 1862, which they wore during the Peninsular Campaign. Partly because these made excellent

targets, the unit lost 228 men during that campaign.

50. The New York State jacket had a slash-type breast pocket. State infantry regiments numbered 1-105 received these jackets which were made with sky-blue trim. Red trim went on the jackets issued to the first four state artillery regiments. These jackets proved highly popular, and men from regiments not issued with them still managed to obtain and wear them.

 50▲ 51▼

52▲

51. Pennsylvania issued plain, dark-blue jackets to many of its men. This man wears such a jacket, and he has decorated the chinstrap of his forage cap with the brass numbers and letters '50 PV', for 50th Pennsylvania Volunteers. The 50th served in IX Corps, which saw service along the Carolina coast as well as with the Army of the Potomac.

52. A group of new privates of the 126th Pennsylvania Infantry had themselves photographed in their new, state-issued plain blue uniforms when the unit was mustered in for nine months' service in 1862. This man is one of their number. The regiment saw action at Chancellorsville.

▲53

▲54

53. This rather sad-looking private from Augusta, Maine, wears the standard fatigue uniform of the Union army – a plain, dark-blue blouse fastened down the front with four buttons, sky-blue trousers, and a plain, dark-blue cap with a varnished black leather peak and chinstrap and brass side buttons.

54. The issue fatigue blouse came with one inside breast pocket over the left breast that could be reached without opening the coat. This, however, was not sufficient for everyone. This private, photographed near Harrisburg, Pennsylvania, added to his blouse an outside breast patch pocket, closed with a brass coat button, made of an entirely different material from the coat.

55. The 1861 dress regulations called for dark-, rather than sky-blue trousers, as worn by this man. The polka-dotted bow-tie further indicates that he has been in service only a short time. His sky-blue overcoat is on the chair next to him, topped by his fatigue cap with a company letter 'A' and regimental number.

56. Enlisted men, like officers, often preferred custom-made versions of the fatigue blouse. This hospital steward wears such a blouse, with two side pockets and one breast pocket. He holds a narrow-brimmed slouch hat. His green half chevrons edged with yellow, bearing a caduceus in the centre, indicate his grade. He was photographed in Harrisburg, Pennsylvania.

57. This Lewisburg, Pennsylvania, sergeant wears another version of the custom-made fatigue blouse. He also has three pockets on the outside and sky-blue chevrons on each sleeve. He wears a dark-blue military-style waistcoat, as well.

58. Private Alister M. Grant, a 'gentleman' from Philadelphia by profession, shows the uniform he wore as a member of Landis' Pennsylvania Battery during the Gettysburg campaign – complete with mud on the trouser legs. The militia battery members wore light-grey slouch hats with red hat cords, and fatigue blouses with five buttons on the front.

59. This private from Bordentown, New Jersey, wears a long version of the custom blouse that was apparently uniform to his regiment. A III Corps member, his cap badge is hidden under the rubber rain cover over his forage cap. This cover fastened to the side buttons and fitted snugly over the rest of the cap, leaving only the peak revealed.

60. The 36th Illinois Infantry was distinguished by the unit's unique cap badge, the regimental numbers within a wreath, as worn on the front of this private's forage cap. The sky-blue waistcoats with eighteen or so small brass buttons were also unique to Illinois troops. The 36th, a IV Corps member, lost 739 officers and men during the war.

▲61

61. Bandsmen, such as these from Quakertown, Pennsylvania, often wore versions of the fatigue blouse with shoulder insignia like that worn by officers, although they were not commissioned. The original print of this picture shows the top of the horn player's forage cap to have been coloured red as were the shoulder-straps.

62. The officer's dark-blue overcoat had four black silk buttons and loops across the front and a cape that could be detached. Rank was indicated on the cuff; a plain cuff, such as that worn by this man from Jersey City, was for a second lieutenant.

▲62

63▲

64▲ 65▼

63. Captain John H. Symonds, 22nd Massachusetts Infantry, was commissioned on 1 October 1861 and discharged on 26 August 1863. He wears a unique belt-plate which bears the state's coat of arms and shows the black quilted cotton lining in the officer's overcoat. The 22nd served with the Army of the Potomac's V Corps, in the Peninsula, Fredericksburg, Chancellorsville and Gettysburg.

64. The single black braid on this officer's cuff indicates that he is a first lieutenant, while the

silver letters 'US' within a gold wreath indicate that he is a staff officer. Each higher rank had an additional cuff braid, up to five for a colonel, so that a major's cuff would have three braids.

65. The enlisted foot soldier's sky-blue overcoat had a cape that ended at the elbow. The sleeves were made longer than necessary to serve as mittens, but could be folded up for convenience. Notice the side this infantryman's dress hat is looped up on.

▲67

66. The standing collar on the foot soldier's overcoat could be worn folded down; it was of the thickness of several pieces of cloth and tended to chafe the neck. This man is also wearing a watch-chain with his sky-blue, military-style waistcoat and a rather plain slouch hat.

67. Although the sky-blue trousers and dark-blue kepi on this man indicate that he is a soldier, his waistcoat and shirt are strictly civilian. Such white or colour checked shirts, usually red or blue, were quite common because most soldiers preferred to purchase shirts or have them sent from home rather than wear the grey flannel issue shirts of poorer quality.

68. Captain William B. Shubrick, Chairman of the Navy's Lighthouse Board during the Civil War, wears the dress coat for an officer of his rank, according to the 1852 regulations. He should also have worn dress trousers with a gold stripe down each leg. Only top-ranking Navy officers continued to wear epaulettes during the war.

69. Commander John L. Worden, who commanded the USS *Monitor* in its history-making fight with the CSS *Virginia*, wears the rank insignia style made regulation in July 1862 (until May 1863), with its combination of broad and narrow gold bars around each cuff. Worden also commanded the USS *Montauk* when she sank the CSS *Nashville* on 28 February 1863.

▲70

70. Since rank insignia regulations changed several times during the war there was often a mixture of different types to be seen at once. This commander wears a coat with the executive star over gold lace bars, one for each grade, authorized in May 1863. His hat, however, features the wide gold band and cap badge with an eagle within a wreath authorized in 1852.

71. Straw hats were authorized, and widely worn in hot climates by Navy officers. This officer, photographed after May 1863, would rate as a lieutenant commander, but the executive star is missing, indicating that he is a civil officer, either a surgeon, paymaster, chief engineer, naval constructor (less than five years' service), a chaplain (less than fourteen years'), or a professor of mathematics (less than twelve years').

▲71

72. The leaf design between two bars in the shoulder-straps, together with the two narrow cuff stripes without an executive star indicate that this officer, photographed in Gibraltar after May 1863, is an assistant paymaster. Because of that area's hot climate, he wears authorized white trousers and a detachable white cap cover.

73. The Navy had a number of warrant officer ranks whose equivalent in the Army would have been somewhere between commissioned and non-commissioned officers. One such rank was that of master's mate, who could command some types of small boat. This master's mate, photographed after May 1863, is distinguished by his lack of shoulder-straps, the cap badge consisting of a plain wreath, and a single star on his cuffs. Note the regulation Navy officer's sword.

▲74　▼75　　　　　　　　　　　76▶

74. Midshipmen were distinguishable by the two fouled anchor badges worn on the collar. Like all officers, they were authorized to wear short blue jackets, but these were mostly worn at the Naval Academy and were abandoned on active service. This midshipman's cap has been covered with a rubber waterproof cover. His overcoat is on the chair next to him.

75. From 1852, clerks, such as this man, were to wear single-breasted coats with falling collars and a single row of six buttons down the front. Caps featured a plain wreath for a badge. A clerk was considered to be a warrant officer. The shape of the cap, with very little overhang, and its lack of a gold stripe, suggests a post-May 1863 date for this photograph.

76. The comfortable sack coat, copied from coats worn by civilian businessmen, became a standard, if unauthorized, sea dress for most Navy officers. It was finally authorized officially on 14 January 1865. It was usually worn with cuff insignia and shoulder-straps. The lack of such insignia, and the gold cap lace in this photograph suggests that the subject was a master's mate, some time from July 1862 to May 1863.

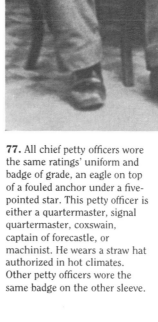

77. All chief petty officers wore the same ratings' uniform and badge of grade, an eagle on top of a fouled anchor under a five-pointed star. This petty officer is either a quartermaster, signal quartermaster, coxswain, captain of forecastle, or machinist. He wears a straw hat authorized in hot climates. Other petty officers wore the same badge on the other sleeve.

78. Dress of seamen, such as these two shipmates, was copied from that of the Royal Navy and consisted of dark-blue pullover shirts, plain trousers, and peakless caps. A black handkerchief was worn around the neck, often buttoned down under two small tabs on the front of the collar. A wide flap, often decorated with white stripes and stars, covered the back of the neck.

▲79 ▼80

▲81

82▲

83▲

79. The dress of US Marine Corps officers was similar to that worn by Army officers, save that all ranks wore double-breasted coats with gold Russian shoulder-knots with the rank insignia in silver on top of them, such as this worn by Lieutenant Mews, USS *St. Mary's*, a sailing sloop in the Pacific Fleet. Coats and French-type kepis were dark-blue; trousers were sky-blue with a red stripe down each leg.

80. The dress of Marine Corps enlisted men, such as this private, included a dark-blue, double-breasted coat with a standing collar with two yellow lace buttonholes, the whole edged with red piping; a brass fringed shoulder-scale on each shoulder (this man has removed his and the attachments for them are visible); and two yellow slash buttonholes on each cuff. For undress, an Army-type forage cap with a gold buglehorn around a silver Old English 'M' on a red crown was worn.

81. Lieutenant Jerry J. Benson served in the US Revenue Marine Cutter Service from 1843 until 1846. He was commissioned a second lieutenant in the Service on 12 November 1861 and was promoted to first lieutenant on 11 July 1864. His uniform is similar to that worn by Navy officers, except that the cap badge features a fouled anchor over the Treasury Department shield within a wreath. The Service was controlled by the Treasury Department in time of peace; by the Navy in wartime.

82. Volunteer militia units made up the bulk of America's military might in 1861. Virtually every town, no matter how small, had one of these outfits, which uniformed themselves according to their pleasures and pocketbooks. This lieutenant is from Worcester, Massachusetts. Militia units from that state often preferred grey uniforms, considering blue to be reserved for the regular army.

83. During the Civil War New Jersey raised its own Rifle Corps for local defence. For field purposes, Corpsmen wore plain grey jackets and trousers and had grey caps with black bands. Dress uniforms included blue jackets cut in the chasseur style, slightly longer than zouave jackets, with slits on each side.

▲84

84. Large cities had literally dozens of volunteer militia units, often quite old, each with a more eleborate dress than the next. This man's unit is unknown, although he was photographed in New York City. But his uniform, with its fringed worsted epaulettes, three rows of gilt buttons, cap with a pompom and the letters 'ER' within a wreath, white waist-belt, and lighter trousers with two stripes down each leg, is typical of many volunteer uniforms.

85. Uniforms worn by units raised immediately before the Civil War, when the forthcoming war was becoming obvious, were often much plainer than those worn by older units. This New Yorker of an unidentified unit, wears a very modern-style frock-coat decorated only by three buttonholes on each cuff and a small single button on the standing collar.

▲85

86. Mounted units were less common than foot units among the volunteer militia. Horses and their equipment simply cost too much for many volunteers. This Harrisburg, Pennsylvania private, however, belongs to a mounted militia unit whose short jackets had their collars decorated with a false buttonhole with a button on each end.

87. One of the most noted of all pre-war volunteer militia units was the First Troop, Philadelphia City Cavalry, founded in 1775. The unit saw short spells of active service on several occasions during the War. This Trooper wears the dark-blue dress coat with its red cuffs and standing collar, white lace, and silver-and-red sash. His Tarleton helmet, with its silver trim and black plume, is on the table next to him.

The *Fotofax* series

A new range of pictorial studies of military subjects for the modeller, historian and enthusiast. Each title features a carefully-selected set of photographs plus a data section of facts and figures on the topic covered. With line drawings and detailed captioning, every volume represents a succinct and valuable study of the subject. New and forthcoming titles:

Warbirds
F-111 Aardvark
P-47 Thunderbolt
B-52 Stratofortress
Stuka!
Jaguar
US Strategic Air Power:
  Europe 1942–1945
Dornier Bombers
RAF in Germany

Vintage Aircraft
German Naval Air Service
Sopwith Camel
Fleet Air Arm, 1920–1939
German Bombers of WWI

Soldiers
World War One: 1914
World War One: 1915
World War One: 1916
Union Forces of the American
  Civil War
Confederate Forces of the
  American Civil War
Luftwaffe Uniforms
British Battledress 1945–1967
  (2 vols)

Warships
Japanese Battleships, 1897–1945
Escort Carriers of World War Two
German Battleships, 1897–1945
Soviet Navy at War, 1941–1945
US Navy in World War Two, 1943–1944
US Navy, 1946–1980 (2 vols)
British Submarines of World War One

Military Vehicles
The Chieftain Tank
Soviet Mechanized Firepower Today
British Armoured Cars since 1945
NATO Armoured Fighting Vehicles
The Road to Berlin
NATO Support Vehicles

The *Illustrated* series

The internationally successful range of photo albums devoted to current, recent and historic topics, compiled by leading authors and representing the best means of obtaining your own photo archive.

Warbirds
US Spyplanes
USAF Today
Strategic Bombers, 1945–1985
Air War over Germany
Mirage
US Naval and Marine Aircraft Today
USAAF in World War Two
B-17 Flying Fortress
Tornado
Junkers Bombers of World War Two
Argentine Air Forces in the Falklands Conflict
F-4 Phantom Vol II
Army Gunships in Vietnam
Soviet Air Power Today
F-105 Thunderchief
Fifty Classic Warbirds
Canberra and B-57
German Jets of World War Two

Vintage Warbirds
The Royal Flying Corps in World War One
German Army Air Service in World War One
RAF between the Wars
The Bristol Fighter
Fokker Fighters of World War One
Air War over Britain, 1914–1918
Nieuport Aircraft of World War One

Tanks
Israeli Tanks and Combat Vehicles
Operation Barbarossa
Afrika Korps
Self-Propelled Howitzers
British Army Combat Vehicles 1945 to the Present
The Churchill Tank
US Mechanized Firepower Today
Hitler's Panzers
Panzer Armee Afrika
US Marine Tanks in World War Two

Warships
The Royal Navy in 1980s
The US Navy Today
NATO Navies of the 1980s
British Destroyers in World War Two
Nuclear Powered Submarines
Soviet Navy Today
British Destroyers in World War One
The World's Aircraft Carriers, 1914–1945
The Russian Convoys, 1941–1945
The US Navy in World War Two
British Submarines in World War Two
British Cruisers in World War One
U-Boats of World War Two
Malta Convoys, 1940–1943

Uniforms
US Special Forces of World War Two
US Special Forces 1945 to the Present
The British Army in Northern Ireland
Israeli Defence Forces, 1948 to the Present
British Special Forces, 1945 to Present
US Army Uniforms Europe, 1944–1945
The French Foreign Legion
Modern American Soldier
Israeli Elite Units
US Airborne Forces of World War Two
The Boer War
The Commandos World War Two to the Present
Victorian Colonial Wars

A catalogue listing these series and other Arms & Armour Press titles is available on request from: Sales Department, Arms & Armour Press, Artillery House, Artillery Row, London SW1P 1RT.